LOVE-LINES

Tom Kelly

Red Squirrel Press

First published in the U.K. in 2009
by Red Squirrel Press
PO BOX 219 MORPETH NE61 9AU
www.redsquirrelpress.com

Cover design by Adam Heslop

ISBN 978-1-906700-04-1

Printed in the U.K. by Athenaeum Press Ltd.
Gateshead, Tyne & Wear

Acknowledgements

Thanks are due to the editors of the following
magazines where some of these poems first appeared:

Bare Bones, Borderlines, Chanticleer, Community of Poets, Curlew, Envoi, Fire, Headlock, Here Now, Iota, Iron, Moodswing, Noises from The Isle, Oasis, Other Poetry, Penniless Press, Pennine Ink, Poetry Nottingham, Poetry Scotland, Pulsar, Purple Patch, Vigil, Red Herring, Retort, Sand, Seafield Poetry Calendar, Sepia, Slipstream, Stand, The Affectionate Punch, The Interpreter's House, The Yellow Crane.

And in the ezines
http://www.interpoetry.com
www.concelbratory.blospot.com/
http://www.aireings.co.uk/Issue2/2_magazine.htm
http://jameskirkup.com/AND/vol1.html

And in the following publications:
Still with Me, (Aquila); John Donne In Jarrow (Here Now); In The Distance, (KT Publications); That Time Of Life, (KT Publications); The Picture From Here, (Sand Press).

And to my brother Terry Kelly for his
invaluable advice on the collection.

Finally to my family Linda, Bethan,
Fiona and Adam with all my love.

Contents

The Letter He Didn't Write
(From Tommy Kelly in a German Prisoner Of War Camp, to his sons, daughter and grandchildren)

I've told you some stories, that's what they're not.
Picture what I say, hold the cold,
put your hand in ice,
fridge will do.

What's worse is not knowing.
It's like that all the time.

Have you got your hand in the fridge?

I prayed for an end. Stop.
My life on pause.

They're all here: French, English, Taffs, Scots,
Geordies like me. Nobody understands us.

I saw the French eat a crow. God, did it squawk.
Never seen anything like that.

Did I tell you about that French officer?
I found him. Hung himself.
In the toilets. Nowt to live for.
That's how it gets you. Scrapes away hope,
stomach knotted.

How's your hand in that fridge?
You've got another five years.

'Carry On' In A Prisoner of War Camp

I am annoyed. I want to ask so much,
why are you wearing your uniform
in the prisoner of war camp?
How did the uniform survive? Did you not grow?
Captured at nineteen, two more years
to grow in and out the bloody thing.
You are at the end of the line,
a daft grin. Grinning
in a Stalag bloody camp. Come on.
This is getting more like,
'Carry On' in a prisoner of war camp.
Is that Sid James in the front row?
Give me a break. I'll re-read your story,
a Frenchman hung himself, you found him,
other prisoners ate crow.
Not this bloody laughing.

Old Soldiers Never Cry

Give me another shot,
don't put that gun to my head,
let me have a fighting chance
not a backs-to-the-wall
arse-nipped-in-and-sweating-buckets-life.

Give me another go,
be fair, let me travel the full journey
without once checking my change,
dodging the inspector,
hoping I don't have to hit the tracks.

Give me another chance,
better innings,
batting average up,
look up now and again,
see a clear sky,
ball flying into blue yonder.

Give me a try,
don't let me slip at first base,
fall on my face, have the rest
trample me underfoot,
let me look to the stars.

Chekhov's Grandfather

Dad never bought his freedom,
he was a serf:
labouring jobs, bottom of the pile,
low self-esteem c.v.

Always in the 1930's,
like Anton he had a hacking cough.

I say, "Chekhov's grandfather was a serf…"
You walk away
to the club,
didn't know him,
never drank together,
your back seems to say.

Another Night With The Photograph Album
1.

Your arm circled the plate
protecting food,
making sure you got it all.

Five years in a prisoner of war camp
made you careful
food became everything: if you don't eat
you won't live.

The shape of your arm
makes me see a sculpture,
strong image,
for you it was another day alive.

2.

You cup a burning cigarette in the palm of your hand,
a mantle with a flesh lampshade that glows by your side,
you leg it to the pub, eyes intent, fixed on a pint,
smoky room, somebody singing in the corner, piano player vamping
somewhere near the melody, like your life: not quite right,
it didn't work out, calculations went awry, shadows
slid over your eyes too often, you got it wrong, somehow.

3.

The oxygen mask shells your mouth as your eyes dodge
round the hospital room, asking questions
as we read the doctor's notes and you, our reactions,
before greyness crept in.

I see us kicking a football on a field, I want to say,
but it'll seem odd, signal I'm cutting into the past,
placing you there, giving you no future, so I say nothing
but lies, "You'll be all right...wait and see". You see through me
as if I'm made of glass.

4.

I recall your story from the prisoner of war camp:
you and your mate threw hot water at the soup queue,
they screamed and you cupped your fill, desire
for life, strong as a mule, near the end
you couldn't eat anything.

5.

You smile from the photograph, reveal your bronzed chest,
don't blink at the sun, have you ever been so happy?
And now no one says, "sorry,"
it's been over a year, and no-one asks,
"What was the matter?" And no one says, "Was he bad for long?"
No one stops my mother, asks about my father.
You smile and the sun's shining, the evidence in my hands.

6.

I don't want to remember rain,
times we fought over whatever,
dog-eared days, rights and wrongs, digging the dirt...

There was pain, shouting, blows and threats,
you smashing a toy, me crying, promising, digging my fingers
into my palms, I'd never speak to you again,
the same meals and poverty
you could taste, so tangible, my children can't even dream of the lack,
and is there any value in picking at scabs that have healed long and
faraway ago and I'm not going to kill you with sainthood,
I'm trying to make sense of this.

7.

I shove to the back of my mind the visits: hospital wards, lolling
bodies, the smell you forget until the next time.
I can't erase your stare, hoarse whispering, desperate attempts to say,
"I'm frightened...I don't want to die" and we knew you were and
avoided the inevitable by smiling, telling jokes and
talking about football as time fell asleep and your eyes aped the clock
and we ran into the dark, rain spreading our tears.

Another death, another night in the Chapel of Rest, another funeral,
another, "I'm sorry" but this time it's you and the photograph album
breaks from its binding and wings it, memories flying,
you want to make them live, walk into the room, go to the bar,
right a few wrongs, but no, I can't because you are dead,
memories can't breathe, that's it.
Photographs umbrella the light but stop a long way short of living.

Same Old Story

This is about you,
loop tape refusing
to snap, spool away.

Dreaming about you,
words splutter on
and tonight
I heard your voice.

I see you
out the corner of my eye,
smell your labourer's sweat.

You stand perfectly still
for once
no stutter
eyes confident
before life
spat you out
left you high and try
as you might
it was the same old story.

Tell Me

I'm searching for you
dewdrop on the end of your nose
wanting to be somewhere else
tangible,
me not knowing what you had suffered.

Tell me what you know,
not this introspective guessing I'm going in for,
whisper in my ear
not silence
I had to contend, not deal with,
just tell me.

Dead ten years,
you can do better than silence
I've never learned to lived with,
I deserve more,
want more
than following men,
strangers like me and you,
an epitaph I don't want.

Dad And Frank O'Hara

In the loo with dad
at the trough, music being piped and
him dead embarrassed in this nearly-posh bar.

I said nothing to anyone
-except you, Frank O'Hara.
I'd just read your poems,
your uncollected:
saw you in NYC,
dad joined us.

Next thing
dad and me are drying our hands in unison,
the drier masks our one-sided conversation,
something you would approve of,
not that I'm seeking approval
just telling you, dad and Frank
are with me
as water flushes away and music
pipes on.

Kiss

Tonight I kissed my dead father
in my sleep;
he was a reclining Christ,
eyes closed,
skin young, pewter-like.

Tonight I kissed my dead father
in my sleep,
he had turned to stone,
surprised by his metamorphosis,
flying above the flat roofs of Lukes Lane Estate,
long-gone Monkton Cokeworks,
headed for immortality
somewhere near the Elmfield Club.

Tonight I kissed my dead father
in my sleep;
silent as stone he had become,
needing a shave,
adhesive for his false teeth.

Tonight I kissed my dead father
in my sleep;
I tried not to remember but he followed me
pointing his long bony finger,
as I threw back the duvet,
remembered that kiss
I had never given him in life.

Combing My Father's Hair

making his high forehead
Mekon-like.

The mirror distorts features,
giving him different glasses
doesn't help.

In the background someone's singing
George Formby songs.
I push dad's white-straw hair
the wrong side,
give him a parting he's never had.

With Her Son

My mother's following me
in the crowd,
I look behind, she's there
cutting a swath through the foyer
into my footsteps,
not knowing where she's going
happy to be travelling with her son

Boxing Day Call

and there's an empty ring
to her voice,
she wants to say, "I'm lonely...
seen no-one, not spoken to a sinner..."

TV's on, loud, day and night.

She's all right, she says,
must talk to someone,
see if they're coping.
She's not.

Bare Wires

A drum thunders in her stomach.
Getting by is a struggle.
She wants the telephone to ring when she's not crying.
She needs everything to be better.
She sees hope in nothing.

She can't touch anything
without being sick.

She feels the bare wires
in her thin wet hands.

Blame

My mother can’t breathe,
hands grope air.

We open windows
she shouts,
blaming everyone.

We rewrite history
make a life
easily packaged,
blemishes removed, painted over.

Make a list: poverty
spending
what you will never have,
chances squandered.

Chasing Away A Wasp

She wonders
always,
can't recall the moment
this
or that happened,
her hands flutter
chasing away a wasp.

Then she cries
fleeing down corridors,
with a collar of doubt
that tightens.

Rare

Half-ten in the morning,
she's watching staff,
hoping for movement:
washing dishes, changing beds,
helping by being there.

We say we're clearing her house,
mention the death of her cousin and
she responds, dullness evaporating,
recalling his Jimmy Cagney ways,
we laugh together: a rare change.

Dog Biscuits

She's got her Larry the Lamb voice on
or Beckett pauses
depending on the day
or night you ring her.

The doctor's weary
of being called out,
she goes to the surgery,
gets antibiotics.

"Big as dog biscuits",
she says.

Mam And The Dog

"I bet that dog's sick as a pig",
mam says,
seeing a dog being taken for a drag,
wanting to be somewhere else,
this constitutional not for it.

Does she see herself in the dog?
Her son and his car, her lead
to nowhere she wants to go.

Her face reveals little
dull mask
fixed on a distant dog.

Come To This

Waving from a window,
handkerchief flagging
us down the path and away,
it's not until later
that it hits me,
her flag of truce
she would have never allowed.
I don't cry,
it's come to this
after all the tears.

For Ages And Ages

she remains staring at the serrated abyss
of her sagging, open-mouthed bag.

I don't know what she's looking for,
an animal burrowing,
I want it to stop,
she's on constant replay.

Over and over,
the same set of questions,
you hardly have time to answer
before the next round
hits you and it goes on
for ages and ages.

In Hospital

We stood round your bed, our wives at the door
as if that's as near as they should be
to your passing, to your death.

"It'll not be long," the sister said.
No one said, "die".

We held your hands,
you grasped ours.

Old People's Friend

All those false alarms:
hospital visits, always, it seems, during the early hours,
"I'm dying," you said, time after time.

All those false alarms:
grasping air as if strangling yourself,
screaming at everyone, the world to blame.

All those false alarms:
heart attacks that were and weren't,
asthma attacks, ditto.

All those false alarms:
running in hospitals,
patient nurses, untouchable consultants.

All those false alarms:
dementia was your cross
you bore, as with everything, badly.

All those false alarms:
spitting recriminations,
hurtful to everyone in sight.

Old people's friend
pneumonia,
the final false alarm
we all saw coming
from a mile off.

In Adoration

In my dream you are at a bus stop,
huddling together with my aunts,
eyes miles away,
you're not speaking because I've not heard
your worries, you've been telling the tale,
I haven't been all ears, you don't say.

A car's leaving the station, heading
for eternity, nothing new in that.

The sun has us snipers:
narrow-eyed, bowing
in adoration to grief.

Mam and Sharon Olds's *'The Father'*

Sharon says, "Do you think you didn't bond?"
Mam answers with a question,
"Was ya dad bad for long?"

Sharon begins to answer but is startled by tears,
mam gives her a mug of warm white wine
she drinks without pulling a face.

This is mam's living room: wobbly coffee table,
boxes of pills, doctors' prescription notes for more
of the same, romantic novel, large print, from the library.

Sharon describes, in detail, her father's death:
the hair up his nose, colour of his stools.
Mam says, "Don't talk to me about shite,
aa could write aa book about it".
Sharon says, "I will".

I Had To Stop Myself

ringing,
my mobile a gun I was going to fire,
tell you my news.

The window's open, blinds rattle.
I was going to ring, your number
touching my fingertips,
your face opposite me,
you were sitting on a brown plastic chair,
disgruntled over something,
I almost spoke to kill the near-silence.

The radiators cold as clay,
footsteps on the stairs,
regimented, a slow march to you.

The Key

There was a key in your drawer,
among breadcrumbs, torn envelopes.
I never discovered where it belonged,
what it fitted,
opened, closed.

“Doing The Tennessee Wigwalk”

Grandmother had crushed ankles,
empty wooden bowls,
walked with a “wiggle and a waddle”.

Grandfather hit her with a stick,
caused the damage.

Women had a place,
had to be quick
not to walk
with a “wiggle and a waddle,”
thirty years later.

Pot Of Gold

Lighting a coal fire, first in years,
I remember sitting with my grandmother,
hunched conspirators staring at coals,
telling tales, saying strangers
would be coming, flakes fluttering
meant money.
"It might be your Uncle John in America"
she'd never heard from for fifty years,
"Maybe that's where the pot of gold's coming from,
you never know." She smiled knowingly.
Even then I knew.

Grandmother Tells Her Tale

standing by the front door
to anyone that happens to pass.
She wants a life of sorts,
I sit by her side, watch, listen.

Picture the child sitting Buddha-like,
knowing nothing but a cold step.
She searches for something beyond this,
I sense her need.

I wish then and now I could help,
useless, providing only company.
Granda, hunched in front of TV,
shouts, "another loser".

She lost two children in childbirth,
one at fifteen with TB: she was used to losing.

You And The Rent Man

Under the tablecloth a rent book,
pound notes inching out, like stiff tongues,
licking my hungry eight-year-old eyes.

The Rent Man was important,
you put your make-up on for him,
smiled whatever he said.
You could hear the jingle of his money bag
as he John Wayne-d up the street.

Granny

in the shipyard,
heavy metal drill
in her right hand,
its point touching the ground
as it scrapes along
beside her for two or three paces
until she hauls it
like a baby over your shoulder.

A lady driller,
she's proud of that,
badge of honour:
not Maggie, mother,
wife, daughter, but worker
trailing her drill
across sodden shipyard floors.

She held the image all her life,
different from this,
she'd not say
her hands lost in soapy water.

Into Mourning

You were smaller than I remember;
your body pinched,
didn't look me in the eye.

Wearing washed-out grey,
as if frost was breaking up on you,
shuffling,
heading to the fire.

I was breaking into day:
alarm on the horizon,
radio chattering
but for a moment you were there.

I walked away from you
into mourning
thirty years ago.

A Letter From James Robert Henderson
Aboard The Wellesley, on the River Tyne, 14th March, 1907.

Me Mother placed me on this training ship,
she cannit look after me.
Ah'm writing this letter with aa thick black vine,
letters tak' ower th' paper.

Today wi scrubbed th' deck in tha rain,
hands hard with tha' months aa've bin heor.

They tell us ta pray,
aa pray ye'll think of me.

Ya grandfather to-be, James Robert Henderson,
aged eight, this day.

Bare Bones
(The Training Ship, Wellesley, burnt on the Tyne, 1914)

I've got this photograph,
your steely stare,
grandfather dutiful as a young soldier
by your stiff side.

No maternal arm round your son.
No smile for the camera.
No laugh at the sky.
No thanks for the memory.
No please come back I'll make things right.

Your story, the bare bones, is all I have:
unmarried mother, worked in a factory,
sent her son, my grandfather,
on a training ship,
"couldn't handle him".

New Year's Day

"And if you go to the Pit Heap,
you'll see a man with as many noses as days in the year",
grandfather said.

I saw furtive men chasing dogs,
men who had lost something
but I didn't know what
as they stumbled over coal traces.

I stood on the bleak corner,
grey as death and worried
that I'd meet the man with as many noses
as days in this new year.

Grandfather Entertaining

The back room,
fire bubbling
the side of the piano.

You pummelling keys
as if making bread.

Your left hand vamping,
right struggling
to find melody.

The tune's recognised,
curtains closed,
fire dampened down.

In The Distance

Granda could tie knots,
his fingers amazed
as they blurred and stopped
revealing a sculpture.

That moment was magical,
halted my breath.

He'd smack his pipe
look in the distance,
hand over the beautiful keepsake
without looking.

Tot

The lads in the yard
christened you 'Tot.'
You preferred James Robert,
saying it slowly with pride.

You lie in hospital
for the last time.

An old mate
dying opposite
stage whispers,
"Poor Tot".
The screens
were round him first.

I Watch

my dead grandfather singing in the bar,
his one suit glistening.

The barmaid wears a benign
clip-on smile.

I should have bought him a pint,
took him home,
depending on my arm,
steer him to bed.

I watch him sing,
walk home alone.

Some Saint's Life

The ceiling's high as I can imagine
except when I fly, but that's different.

I see the headmaster, his hair precise,
suit, shoes, neat.

The small log cane
hits my hands
they scream, go cold, pulse,
I sit on them,
listen to the teacher
tell us of some saint's life.

1952

And a photograph holds time
and a photograph keeps a memory
and you look at this black and white duo
and you try to recall
and you examine the image closely
and there is nothing
but two characters
smiling for whatever reason
back at you
from a past
that was you.

Loved Ones

Don’t break the toy
in my dream, not this time.

Don’t scream, fight
on the excuse for a carpet.

Don’t take my money
I hid and saved.

Don’t let me feel
pain that burns.

The Best Years Of Your Life

Gangsters, just out of short trousers,
pressing stolen chocolates in my face,
pissing in milk bottles,
telling lies about girls;
fighting, biting
hating teachers:
sniffing friends and enemies.

I see them sometimes
fatter, bald, drunk,
genial, surly:
I remember not to remember.

Ignorant

Sticklebacks do forty-five degrees
with each flick;
frog spawn congeals
under the damp, shadowy bridge.

We step on stones,
stilt walkers,
sprites in bare feet,
reflections walking on air
laughing up the cemetery bank
carrying our socks on shoulders.

I was dad in the POW camp,
my tongue dry as sticks,
his like leather,
as he sucked snow.

We use sticks as guns,
ignorant of what our fathers endured.

Photograph

I don’t recognise him:
navy blue suit, white shirt,
black and diamond speckled tie,
and the speech;
snow making him say,
“Welcome to Omsk”.
A joke he probably loved.

I don’t recognise him
but feel for that young man
mistakes, hurt, love he’s given.

I don’t recognise him
know him,
wonder what other paths
he could have explored
what answers he could have found
looking at my photograph

Wrapped Round Me

The call for you came at one in the morning:
silent taxi, singing roads,
maternity hallways, pilots of light,
signalling your birth.

Sealed in an incubator:
unaware of fear, distant slamming doors,
television chained in the empty waiting room.

I listen for any sound to recall,
in some future.
I wait for whatever night decides to bring,
the umbilical cord of enduring love,
wrapped round me forever.

Velvet Sleep

I want the all day buffet of sleep,
return time and again, without broken dreams.
Then more, a full course meal of eight hours,
uninterrupted snoring.
The duvet tastes so sweet,
good enough to eat,
lie all day.

Don't let me go struggling to your crying cot,
my hand swimming through those wooden bars,
hearing your cry subside as I sleep standing up.

I want to eat, drink, devour sleep,
breakfast, dinner, tea.
I am deprived, crying, whinging in a corner.

I want to throw myself on the floor, curl up,
become a child, yes become you, a baby,
give me your gentle movement, your velvet sleep.

Boxed-Out

This is the moment when the world is boxed out:
front door locked, chain hanging like a droopy eye.
Before ten, asleep in your cot,
checked on you seven times.

You are our perfect answer,
we laugh at nothing,
suck lemons,
lose smiles,
stop our jaws aching.

I Want You To Know

your mother wanted you more than anything,
you were the most important thing in her life.

I know the precise moment we wanted you,
how we imagined you were a boy,
called you 'Ned', then you were born nameless.

I want to tell you she loved you,
with a frightening intensity.

I want you to be with her,
would love her to feel this moment,
walk with you now.

Time In The Yard

Playing in the yard,
studying bricks,
inching baby fingers
against brick and mortar,
cut-down warrior
with milk bottle legs
in the sun.

You throw your hat,
it sails,
caught on a sudden breeze,
and you are here,
six-year-old,
no longer a baby,
reading without your finger,
eating with knife and fork,
including me in your stories,
playing with time in the yard.

Hurt You

Everyday balancing practicalities
spinning plates
above my head,
feeling tension
aware they could fall
smash on the floor
have me scrabbling
among china shavings,
that may pierce your feet
cut into your soft soles
hurt you in any way at all.

Your Drawings

You've given me a smile like a red banana,
glasses and stubble are missing.
In your drawings, greyness is abolished,
we stare ahead, hiding nothing,
in your world we smile more than anything.

To Fiona

The breeze
presses your hair against your forehead,
waves the swimming pool
you are diving in.

The watery sun
you are ignoring with laughter
smirks through clouds,
highlights your face
making sad shadows.

My anxiety
runs to you,
seems to love fear
you cannot feel or see.

In The Dark

Don't be afraid
as you scurry from your room
into ours,
looking at the drifting curtains,
shadows on the ceiling.

In you, I see me,
running with fear.

Don't be afraid,
don't cry
into your pillow,
we are here in the dark.

Dreams

You know one of those anxiety dreams,
when your children
are fighting tigers, you are trapped in a cave
or too far away, can't get near.

You wake, hot, sweating,
confused, half-asleep,
check their bedroom,
to kill a tiger.

Day

Morning frost
runs away
to nothing
on blankets of pavements.

Early evening
car lights
sloosh across roads
climb walls.

Later still
wind hushes
trees
as a child turns restlessly
in her sleep.

Somewhere Else

I open the door
quickly, put on the light,
knowing you're not there.

I'm trying to fool myself,
I know that.

You haven't been abducted by aliens,
joined some religious cult
that stops you speaking to your family,
you are somewhere else.

Not This

This change hits you,
things will never be the same,
grappling hooks on your eyes:
this is how it is.

The past fingers me
has me wanting
the way things were,
not this empty glass of a heart.

You are no longer the child
helping her dad,
you have left me,
with useless memories.

I need the past
take me back.
Hang me beside a day
a dozen years ago
not this.

The Slow Going

She's going to move
and when I see her
I hold the moment.

I know this is what happens,
she needs to leave
grow, make her mistakes.

Tonight, I check her room,
the covers a forced-back eyelid,
bed empty
as my riddled heart.

I Don’t Want You To Go

This leaving I can barely spell or say
packing boxes, filling my car
with you, as tears become razors
and then floor me as I pass your room
and then the gasps of pain, disbelief:
I don’t want you to go.

It’s worse than I imagined or ever wanted to believe,
as I cry at the drop of anyone’s hat,
just ring now and say anything:
I don’t want you to go.

I’m so nervous I have to fight
to do anything.
I watch my mobile phone,
it’s going to explode
if you don’t ring:
I don’t want you to go.

I want you here annoying me
and coaxing and laughing and smiling
telling me that time has stopped
and that we can live in the past
when everything was perfect,
I want to live that lie:
I don’t want you to go.

The Last Winter

Sun's hitting tarmac,
soft to touch.

In the swimming pool
children scream
delight.

The last winter
months away.

October,
cold scuttling in.

November
ice screwed us down.

Christmas beacons a long night.

The last winter
no longer months away.

Alone In The hotel

I don't want to talk
to anyone, however kind.
I hear them.

I want to be here,
nowhere else,
this precise moment.

I'm losing sight of everything.

Our daughter plunders sleep,
her dreams, I hope, happy,
mine sick with fear.

“ The Excellent Will Be Permanent” (Aristotle)

My hand’s in fire.

I’m cut, aching, teeth clamped.
Headache’s fixed,
flagged across my skull.

Clichés inhabit me:
“it takes time”.

You will be remembered,
recalled.
Loss batters me.

My mouth is filled with acid.

Spilt Milk

You're not going to burst through the door,
interrupt my telephone conversation,
say, "sorry," spill coffee on my knees.

You're not going to sit on the telephone for hours
have me half-listening,
pinning lives together
as if they were dress patterns.

You're not going to shout at me,
tell me what I haven't done,
you won't come in the kitchen
where I am crying over spilt milk.

Stupid

I watched a screen,
your name, cause of death,
blinking before me.
The machine copies heartache.

It's stupid
telling a stranger you're dead.
Standing, trying to whisper details
through a window.

"Tell me your story", they all say.
I want to tell them lies.

Wedding Ring

Tapping my finger against a pint glass,
remember my wedding ring's gone.
Drumming the driving wheel,
pushing the ring back and forward
I realise.

At first there was a white band,
exposed flesh for the first time
in twenty-odd years.
Now I can't tell one finger
from another.

Photograph In My heart

Your photograph smiles,
I don't.

Shipped in a compartment
of my wallet,
among credit cards,
crumpled notes.

I could let you go,
see you fly into our house,
nail down windows,
hold you
to my stricken heart.

You

I see you at the mouth of a tunnel,
standing almost perfectly still, a solitary figure
in a black short skirt, white top,
maybe it's a T-shirt, I don't know.

I could have mistaken all of this for a painting,
something primitive,
suggesting a life force.

You remain stationary
until your skirt flutters and you move
to the entrance and it closes behind you.

The Ring

There's a ring in a box,
I see it on your crumpled finger,
ruby red, bold
and you were dying.

There's a memory in that box
and I recall it
fresh as a paper cut,
smarting at the edges.

There's a message
half-finished on a wall,
making no sense,
words abandoned,
for some reason
we will never know.

There's a tangled up dream,
I can't put your finger on the ring,
it moves away
like you.

Mine

Warmth teases out flames of flowers.
I didn't notice them until a pot of yellowness
hit me full in the eyes.

You would have loved to see them,
wouldn't have been a surprise to you,
life-enhancing,
God would have got a mention.
I'm a different kettle of fish,
caught unaware by their gaudiness.

I think of your imagined reactions,
flowers glisten like miniature suns,
nodding, hovering in broken plant pots,
once ours but now all mine.

December And You

Saturday morning: rain steaming off rooftops,
I am numb, deaf, lost.

Greyness wins, my soul's aching, in need of hope
as rain dapples windows.

My heart won't stop haemorrhaging,
I scream as I cut out loss with my bare hands.

I want to see nothing but this black slate roof,
sun climbing in my room and you, you and you.

Dream

Counting the cost is too great:
insidious rain sniggers down,
everything's worse than you imagine.

I never thought this would be me,
this is what happens to someone else.
Sometimes I forget where I am,
retrace my steps as if in a dream.

Picking Strawberries

bending low for those fat ones.

The kids with us are slow learners,
say they've been here dozens of times
when they've been nowhere near anywhere.

These trips cost us,
they haven't got enough money,
never will.

I watched you survey the field
keeping an eye on trouble
that was hitting you.

A year on and strawberries
are there,
kids have been nowhere dozens of times,
you're not in the field
or anywhere.

Most Of The Time

your mother's photograph is alone,
most of the time.
It stares fixedly ahead,
you don't return the smile,
you are not there,
most of the time.

A dozen years have past,
some with barbed wire
in my mouth and crying
is useless as singing at stars,
most of the time.

A bitter wind
signals nothing,
clouds shuffle by,
past is still past,
most of the time.

Dead Telephone

It's the arse-end of April,
could be November,
cats slide indoors,
backs against radiators.

You look forward and back
when months change, seasons slip.

By myself now, I don't like to ring couples,
picturing them wrapped round each other,
wincing at my late-night call.

Telephone's dead: I check to see if it's burring.

I Never Thought

I never thought I'd be visiting like this:
dancing aerosol, water in a bottle.

I never thought I would be at a garage,
buying flowers, carnations you always loved.

I never thought it would be: if I have time,
after work and before another drive home.

I never thought I'd be alone in a car,
a bag of mixed blessings juggling in the boot.

I never thought or believed this would be me,
I imagine that you would feel the same: strange.

I never thought I'd be driving through the gates
and down the shaded path to your graveside.

I never thought there'd be days I'd forget you.
I never thought, I never thought, until now.

Some Scars

never leave,
white line on my toe,
cut on Christmas Day.

Just visible hillock,
on my left hand,
boil when I was eight.

Mark on my forehead,
stone
thrown from a house
being demolished.

You.